Abolishing Man in Other Worlds

ABOLISHING MAN IN OTHER WORLDS

Breaking and Recovering the Chain of Being in C. S. Lewis's Ransom Trilogy

Courtney Petrucci

WIPF & STOCK · Eugene, Oregon

ABOLISHING MAN IN OTHER WORLDS
Breaking and Recovering the Chain of Being in C. S. Lewis's Ransom Trilogy

Wipf & Stock
An Imprint of Wipf and Stock Publishers
199 W. 8th Ave., Suite 3
Eugene, OR 97401

www.wipfandstock.com

PAPERBACK ISBN: 978-1-5326-9392-2
HARDCOVER ISBN: 978-1-5326-9393-9
EBOOK ISBN: 978-1-5326-9394-6

01/11/21

CONTENTS

INTRODUCTION

C. S. Lewis's *The Chronicles of Narnia* is arguably his best-known literary work studied by scholars for decades, but his science fiction Ransom trilogy is gaining more and more attention from academic audiences. The scholarly conversation regarding religion in Lewis's trilogy is different than that of religion in *The Chronicles of Narnia* for multiple reasons. His early science fiction work in *Out of the Silent Planet, Perelandra,* and *That Hideous Strength* demonstrates his belief that Christianity, or earthly religion and worldview, is present in other worlds in outer space. Most of his readers may believe that religion is unique to humans, and without humans to worship their God, religion cannot exist. Without humans, there would be no one to worship a God or watch over God's lower creations. This is certainly not to say that religion does not exist, but there must be humans present in order to have religion in general. Lewis, however, projects humanity into outer space in order to show his readers that religion already exists outside our world, with or without humans. He (along with Tolkien) use their written works to bring their readers back to "dormant convictions and attitudes" such as Christianity, planting seeds in their brains in order to start a "quiet revolution."[1] All Lewis's sentient creatures, including the celestial Oyarses and eldila, worship Maleldil and watch over Maleldil's lower creations as an example of the faith that humans have forgotten.

---

1. Tyson, "Christian Platonism of Lewis and Tolkien," 23.

If we use J. R. R. Tolkien's idea of Recovery (which is discussed in detail in his essay "On Fairy-Stories") as a lens for reading Lewis's science fiction, Lewis's image of Christianity reflects a Recovered version of the Christian worldview. The Space trilogy, in other words, depicts earthly religion as it should be. First, we will briefly look at the trilogy as a whole and explore Lewis's use of the Cosmic Hierarchy of Being, or the Cosmic Chain, in which all beings are interconnected under Maleldil. Then we will discuss how Lewis, whether consciously or subconsciously, draws from WWII for his N.I.C.E. and Un-man characters. We will then turn back to Lewis's religion and decide how his scientists' actions can be classified as "bent" based on how they use their own free wills, and finally explore why C. S. Lewis decided to depict his own religion in outer space. As we will discuss, certain actions by the N.I.C.E. and the Un-man become examples of human self-abolition, which Lewis describes at length in his *Abolition of Man*. Artificially creating our own immortality by abusing eugenics and technology will cause the undoing of our own race. Lewis's characters do so by creating a substitute for the Christian God, and Lewis's message to his readers is to know and accept our given place in the universe.

A BRIEF SUMMARY OF THE TRILOGY

The first two books in the Space trilogy take place on Malacandra (Mars) and Perelandra (Venus), respectively. In *Out of the Silent Planet* (*OSP*), Dr. Elwin Ransom is kidnapped and brought as a human sacrifice to the séroni of Malacandra by Dr. Weston and Dick Devine. Upon their landing on Malacandra, Ransom is able to escape the men, and he spends the next few days wandering through the alien wilderness. He soon meets a new sentient creature called a hross. Ransom is invited back to the hrossa village and over a period of weeks, builds up a companionship with them. They teach each other about their worlds, languages, and cultures, and Ransom learns that the three main Malacandrian races, hrossa, séroni, and pfifltriggi, are able to coexist without violence. The hrossa are skilled poets, the séroni possess logical and practical thinking skills, and the pfifltriggi create tools, architecture, and art.

Weston and Devine eventually find Ransom, but kill Ransom's closest friend, Hyoi, on Malacandra upon their reunion. Whin, another hross, gives Ransom directions to Augray, a sorn who will take Ransom to Oyarsa, and Ransom is again able to evade the two other Earth men. Ransom begins his journey to Oyarsa by going to meet Augray. He teaches Ransom more about who and what Oyarsa is, and we learn that the séroni consider human life to be unguided and "bent" because we "have no eldila" and want to act as our own Oyarses.[1] Finally, Augray brings Ransom to Meldilorn, where Ransom meets the Oyarsa of Malacandra. Ransom learns

---

1. Lewis, *Out of the Silent Planet*, 102.

about the Bent Oyarsa of Thulcandra and how Earth is cut off from the rest of the planets and Oyarses in outer space. Shortly thereafter, Weston and Devine are brought before Oyarsa in a trial concerning Hyoi's murder.

During the trial, Weston explains that he is only concerned with the preservation of humanity. We will discuss this concern much more in depth later, but one of Lewis's central ideas comes out in Weston's defense of his actions. Weston wants to immortalize the human race by invading other worlds and using all the resources available there. Oyarsa finally decides that the three men will return to Thulcandra. Ransom is then given a warning; Oyarsa states that there will be "stirrings and high changes" afoot in Thulcandra,[2] foreshadowing what is to come in *Perelandra*.

Lewis's second book in the trilogy takes place on Venus, or Perelandra. Ransom is given the task of preserving and protecting this young and unfallen planet. His only other human companion is the Green Lady, Tinidril, whom we are able to connect with the biblical Eve because of her pure and unfallen state. She is to be the mother of the planet, and the father will be Tor. Dr. Weston, however, makes a surprise appearance on Perelandra, which sets in motion a chain of events that tests Tinidril's obedience and love for Maleldil. Weston becomes possessed by a bent eldil, and Ransom realizes that his role on Perelandra is to prevent the Un-man, previously Dr. Weston, from defiling Tinidril's devotion to Maleldil. Ransom's battle with the Un-man is at the center of the text, and Ransom succeeds in destroying him before the Un-man can corrupt Tinidril's world.

Tinidril and Tor, mother and father figures on Perelandra, are reunited and raised up as Oyarsa figures as Perelandra gives them dominion over the planet. As they come into their new roles, they invoke what they call the Great Dance, or the beginning of the interrelationships of all beings on Perelandra. They return Ransom to Earth to share his story and begin preparing for the ultimate battle between humanity and the Bent One, which is to take place in the final installment of Lewis's trilogy.

2. Lewis, *Out of the Silent Planet*, 142.

That Hideous Strength (*THS*) focuses on our own planet and human self-destruction. It is set entirely on Earth, and Ransom, though still a main character, takes on a different role. By this time, he is the Head of a group resisting the N.I.C.E., or the National Institute of Co-ordinated Experiments, which aims to create an artificial means of human immortality. They replace the Christian God with something artificial and they endanger the future of humanity by taking away the choice, will, and sentience that makes us human. The Head is hardly human, but the N.I.C.E. considers it a scientific breakthrough in preserving the human race. They essentially intend to destroy humanity and create something inhuman to, ironically, preserve humanity.

The N.I.C.E. also plans to unearth Merlin, whose body is buried in Bragdon Wood, to merge their new-age technological power with his old-world magical powers. They successfully reanimate a scientist's severed head and call it the real God,[3] but they fail to acquire Merlin's help. Upon awakening, Merlin is drawn to Ransom and helps defend the world against the atrocities the N.I.C.E. commits. In addition to Merlin, Ransom also has the help of the Oyarses of the other planets. Malacandra, Perelandra, Viritrilbia of Mercury, Lurga of Saturn, and Glund of Jupiter all descend upon the manor on St. Anne's to help the resistance. Their presence allows the animals doomed to experimentation at Belbury to escape from their cages and retake their places in nature. The N.I.C.E. is dismantled and Earth is liberated from the potential self-annihilation of the human race.

At the close of the *Out of the Silent Planet,* Ransom also learns that the Earth and our Christian God are part of a larger planetary system under Maleldil. Ransom's realization allows us to consider earthly religion as a smaller part of a whole in which the rest of our solar system actively and regularly participates. Earth is a Silent Planet in that it is spiritually disconnected from Maleldil and the other planets because of the Bent Oyarsa. Earth is, on the other hand, simultaneously linked to the rest of the cosmos because so much depends on the outcome of the final battle on Earth in *THS.*

3. Lewis, *That Hideous Strength,* 176.

Lewis returns to our home planet for the last part of his trilogy where the culminating battle between good and evil occurs. With this structure in mind, Lewis first gives his audience a plausible basis for religion as we know it; in other words, Maleldil the Creator is an image of the Christian God, and the idea of religion is only a small piece of Maleldil's actual dominion over our place in the universe. The Creator is in all things in all places in the universe, whether humans acknowledge that presence or not.

DEFINING THE COSMIC HIERARCHY
OF BEING AND THE GREAT DANCE

The most obvious bridge between Lewis's Christian worldview and the worldview in his science fiction is the Hierarchy of Beings. His other worlds reflect the same relationships between creatures as the interrelationships on Earth. Each entity is directly connected to the next in Lewis's cosmic world; that relationship is necessary in order for the universe to function. Each creature has a unique place in the Hierarchy of Beings, but there is also an interrelationship in the chain: Maleldil is the Creator, and as such is outside the chain, but all of Maleldil's creations are underneath him in a hierarchy. The hnau, or rational and conscious beings under Maleldil, serve as Maleldil's messengers and shepherds of non-sentient beings such as animals, plants, and minerals. The hnau, in other words, are Maleldil's link to the smallest creations in nature. The chain of relationships between alien creatures in *OSP* and *Perelandra* mirror those of the Christian, earthly religion. Like Lewis's hnau, humans have dominion over nature and protect God's creations. When Lewis brings his audience back to Earth for *THS*, he presents the interrelationships between humans and the rest of the chain as broken; Ransom and the rest of St. Anne's are tasked with repairing the chain.

In *The Discarded Image*, Lewis explains that all sentient and non-sentient beings, vegetables, minerals, etc. have their own place in the universe. He explains that "everything has its right place, its home, the region that suits it, and, if not forcibly restrained, moves thither by a sort of homing instinct."[1] Naturally, if someone or something tries to move or is moved out of its rightful place, its instinct is to find a way back to that rightful place. Even the planets are in constant motion in the Field of Arbol and are linked to one another by their Oyarses and Maleldil. The Cosmic Chain of Being is a hierarchy that Maleldil created in which all celestial, sentient, and non-sentient beings are in their rightful place.

The Christian God and Maleldil, the Creators, are outside the Chain of Being on Earth and Lewis's other worlds, and beneath them are the Intelligences, or the Guardians. At the top of the medieval Christian chain there are three levels of angels and, though they are given separate levels as if one group of angels is higher or lower than the others, the purpose of their stations in the hierarchy is to show their different roles. As Dionysius explains in *The Celestial Hierarchy*, the Seraphim, Cherubim, and Thrones are closest to God, the Lordships, Powers, and Authorities govern and guide the other celestial beings, and the Angels, Archangels, and Principalities are closest to humans in that they convey messages from God.[2] Lewis's celestial powers are similar, yet there are gaps in the middle level of medieval angels. Lewis's Oyarses are equivalent to the medieval Seraphim as those closest to Maleldil in the chain. They are the "lesser gods" Maleldil assigned to reign over each planet. Paul Fiddes, author of *C.S. Lewis the Myth-Maker*, explains that the Oyarses are equivalent to the guardian angels assigned to different parts of Earth by Yahweh.[3] Sørina Higgins also rightly states that "the Oyarsa is the ruler of the planet and also its spiritual personification or even its soul."[4] They govern and represent their assigned planets. Next are the angels or eldila (equivalent to the Archangels conveying messages from Maleldil to the hnau), the hnau, non-sentient, or the non-hnau beings, and finally vegetable matter and minerals. In *OSP*, Augray, explains this part of the chain to Ransom: "There must be rule, yet how can creatures

1. Lewis, *The Discarded Image*, 92.
2. Pseudo-Dionysius, *Celestial and Ecclesiastical Hierarchy*, 27–36.
3. Ward, *Planet Narnia*, 37.
4. Higgins, "Mythology of the Space Trilogy," 4.

rule themselves? Beasts must be ruled by hnau and hnau by eldila and eldila by Maleldil."[5] According to the Chain of Being, creatures cannot rule themselves.

The interrelationships in the chain depend on each entity helping rule or guide the next, trickling down from God or Maleldil. The chart below demonstrates the parallels between the medieval Christian chain and the chain in Lewis's science fiction from highest in the hierarchy to lowest.

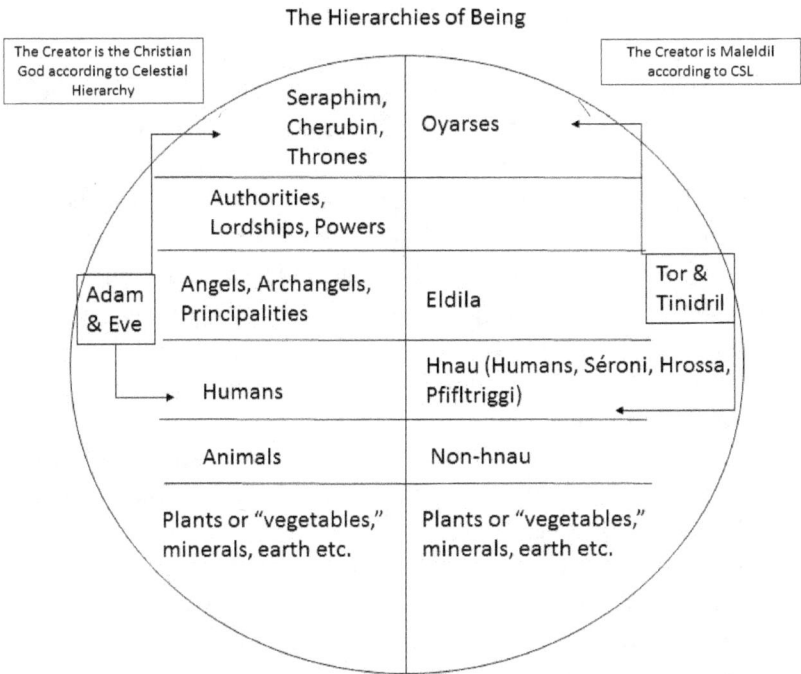

The Hierarchies of Being

The Creator is the Christian God according to Celestial Hierarchy			The Creator is Maleldil according to CSL
	Seraphim, Cherubin, Thrones	Oyarses	
	Authorities, Lordships, Powers		
Adam & Eve	Angels, Archangels, Principalities	Eldila	Tor & Tinidril
	Humans	Hnau (Humans, Séroni, Hrossa, Pfifltriggi)	
	Animals	Non-hnau	
	Plants or "vegetables," minerals, earth etc.	Plants or "vegetables," minerals, earth etc.	

As shown, the left side of the chart represents the medieval model Lewis draws from, and the right represents the Cosmic Hierarchy in his science fiction. God and Maleldil are outside this Chain of Being as the Creators. The Creator cannot be part of the Chain of Being they create because the Creator is not created. This

5. Lewis, *Out of the Silent Planet*, 102.

is the distinction between God and all other created beings.[6] The humans in Lewis's universe attempt to make themselves Creators by providing infinite life for humanity. God gives humans the gift of deification, or the potential to become Gods through obedience as Tor and Tinidril do in *Perelandra*. Humans are tempted to become Gods or godlike on their own as the N.I.C.E. exhibits in their experiments, thus disrupting the Chain of Being. Essentially, God intends to deify us "in his own time," and his creations are not meant to deify themselves or others.[7] Succumbing to such temptation is also disobeying God and causes a disruption of all the other links in the chain. David Downing writes in his *Planets in Peril* that "there is a natural order to everything in nature, and it is a sin if it is tampered with."[8] Of course, this is the entire point of *THS*, where the scientists and N.I.C.E. use other humans for their experiments with immortality. The main conflict throughout this trilogy is the disruption of the Cosmic Hierarchy of Being, the natural relationships between all beings, and it shows a strong connection with some of the evolutionary ideas during World War II, which will also be discussed in a later section. As Lewis develops the Hierarchy of Beings on other planets, he remains consistent with the Christian Cosmic Chain.

The idea of all beings as part of a chain, interrelated and with their own place within that chain, is not a new one. The Cosmic Hierarchy of Being is also depicted as a dance, fluid and continuously moving.[9] Lewis states in *The Discarded Image* that everything has its rightful place or "home," and moves towards it naturally.[10] The celebration at the end of *Perelandra* is an image of the Great Dance, which is essentially the fluid relationship between "beasts, humans, and spirits, [where] all find their place; fallen worlds and unfallen ones, ancient ones and new ones, each participate in the

---

6. Athanasius, *On the Incarnation*, 6–7.

7. Mosley, *Being Deified*, 9.

8. Downing, *Planets in Peril*, 68.

9. Downing, *Planets in Peril*, 46.

10. Lewis, *The Discarded Image*, 92.

pageant."[11] The interrelationships in the chain are fluid in that they each have an effect on the rest of the chain, but the chain itself is static. Lewis also touches upon the Great Dance in his *Discarded Image* in which he discusses the relationships between beasts, the human and rational souls, and the sensitive or vegetable souls.[12] The "Dance" is a relationship or movement that God choreographs for the dancers, or all creatures; each individual is part of a whole and each role is imperative to the functioning of the whole "Dance."

Chapter 17 of *Perelandra* centers around the beginning of the Great Dance on Perelandra. At this point in the text, Ransom is with Perelandra's Oyarsa and Tor and Tinidril, who have just become King and Queen of Perelandra. They are surrounded by an audience of male and female pairs of Perelandrian animals. Tor calls it the beginning of the Great Dance on Perelandra, and over the course of the chapter Ransom experiences multiple visions of the interrelationships of all beings. It is unclear which characters say each section of the dialogue, but Lewis writes that the "Dance," the fluid relationships between beings, events, times, and ideas, has always been present: "We speak not of when it will begin. It has begun from before always. There was no time when we did not rejoice before His face as now. The dance which we dance is at the centre and for the dance all things were made."[13] To further illustrate the fluidity of these relationships, the voice states that there is no equality between beings; the relationships are supportive of one another, interlocking, rather than equal with one another.[14] There is a clear hierarchy with each creature supporting and being supported by the next. In Lewis's fiction, for example, Maleldil rules each planet through the Oyarses, the eldila move amongst the Oyarses and hnau creatures carrying messages, and the hnau creatures (hrossa, séroni, pfifltriggi) work together in stewardship over the non-hnau beings. The "Dance" that occurs on Perelandra is an echo of the Great Dance that takes place throughout the rest

11. Downing, *Planets in Peril*, 46.

12. Lewis, *The Discarded Image*, 146–61.

13. Lewis, *Perelandra*, 183.

14. Lewis, *Perelandra*, 184.

of the universe. The stewardship between beings on Malacandra and Perelandra is again reflective of our own earthly hierarchy in which humans shepherd God's lower beings.

Further, Ransom's experience of the "Dance" on Perelandra, which begins with this series of speeches, changes into a series of visions. He sees all the relationships, like a web, of intertwined individuals. Lewis writes:

> It seemed to be woven out of the intertwining undulation of many cords or bands of light, leaping over and under one another and mutually embraced in arabesques and flower-like subtleties. Each figure . . . became the master-figure or focus of the whole spectacle, by means of which his eye disentangled all else and brought it into unity.[15]

The chain is made up of countless individuals as parts that make up a whole. That whole is the "Dance." The hierarchy is not simply a vertical chain, but a kaleidoscope of interrelated beings that lead to a center. That center is Maleldil, and all things originate from and return back to Maleldil. If we continue to equate Maleldil with the Christian God, religion's natural place in outer space gradually becomes clearer. God, as the Creator of all things, is also present in all things.

15. Lewis, *Perelandra*, 187.

THE REAL "WESTONS"
AND *THE ABOLITION OF MAN*

We must consider what was going on in the world during Lewis's time and what the current events were as he was writing his Space trilogy. The connection between WWII events and Lewis's accomplishment in projecting humanity into outer space yields answers as to religion's place in other worlds. The publication of his three science fiction works spans from 1938 to 1945, during which time Hitler and the Nazis rose to power and exterminated millions of fellow human beings. Sanford Schwartz in his *Final Frontier* states that "Lewis's fighting philologist [Ransom] was conceived in an atmosphere of looming international crisis, and however far he travels from his own planet, the issues surrounding the causes, conduct, and consequences of the Second World War are never far from the surface."[1] *Perelandra* appears when WWII was in its fourth year, and *That Hideous Strength* was released a week before Hiroshima and Nagasaki were bombed. The N.I.C.E.'s goals are to "continue interplanetary expansion; to rid the planet of species that compete with humans for resources; and to purify the human species itself, through 'sterilization of the unfit [and] liquidation of backward races.'"[2] The similarities between these goals and those of the Nazis would have been quite clear to Lewis's 1945 audience. As the worldly current events at the time, it is no

1. Schwartz, *Final Frontier*, 4.
2. Downing, *Planets in Peril*, 55.

surprise that Lewis drew from WWII events, whether consciously or subconsciously.

When one understands the context, it is also no surprise that some of the recurring elements in the Space trilogy are preserving the human race and conquering foreign planets. Readers witness humans experimenting on other humans, both alive and dead, all in search of a means to improve and immortalize the human race. According to Schwartz, Lewis was concerned with the idea of humans taking on subhuman status, or an "evolutionary imperative" to "legitimate the suspension of time-honored ethical norms."[3] Essentially, Lewis's main concern was the disruption of natural human order—not just within the human species, but within human relationships between each other and God.

Lewis recorded his own response to Hitler's actions in his November 5, 1933 letter to Arthur Greeves. He wrote about the evil of Hitler as stupid and cruel.[4] We can assume that Lewis was well-informed since his BBC broadcasts during that time centered around current events. Lewis also wrote to Arthur C. Clarke in 1943 that "a human race concerned only with technological power and with no regard for ethics would be 'a cancer on the universe.'"[5] His comparison between cancer and the obsession with technological progress highlights Lewis's aversion to abusing technological power; it puts into question how our other scientific decisions affect the rest of the universe, but that is a separate argument. It is clear how Lewis draws the connection between the scientific evolution of humanity and the original sin or fall of Adam and Eve. Downing states that "the idea that humans may one day evolve into *Übermensch* was for Lewis the latest variant of the serpent's temptation to Eve: 'Ye shall be as Gods.'"[6] At this time in history and at this point in Lewis's life, with WWII and all its experiments and exploitations of humans, the Cosmic Hierarchy of Being was compromised.

3. Schwartz, *Final Frontier*, 6.

4. Hooper, *War in Deep Heaven*, 126–9.

5. Hooper, *War in Deep Heaven*, 593–4.

6. Downing, *Planets in Peril*, 16. (See also Gen 3:5.)

Not only do Lewis's characters disrupt that natural order, but they also try to find immortality, which Lewis deemed ignorant or "young," as Tinidril says. Schwartz illuminates the connection between Lewis's fiction and historical events by explaining that "these issues were increasingly acute in the early twentieth century, when projects for the 'transformation of humanity' turned from speculative fictions into real-life legislative agendas for the improvement of the species, and at their most extreme, into lethal crusades to secure the future of the evolutionary process itself."[7] Specifically, one of the Nazi objectives was to manipulate the process of human evolution, making a master race, thus changing the relationships between those humans and the rest of the Cosmic Hierarchy.

At this time in history, Scientism flared up in popularity only to be quenched again when news of experiments on humans in concentration camps was exposed to the general public.[8] Scientism is "the belief that the supreme moral end is the perpetuation of our own species, and that this is to be pursued even if, in the process of being fitted for survival, our species has to be stripped of all those things for which we value it."[9] Testing on humans and animals, euthanasia, and sterilization were some of the areas that were endorsed for experimentation in the early twentieth century in the US and Europe in order to find ways of improving our species.[10] It is no coincidence that Lewis includes most of these things in *THS*. Lewis feared that allowing science to carry out such unethical experiments in the US and Europe would cause those governments to follow the Nazi example, devaluing and jeopardizing human life.[11] His Ransom trilogy presents Scientism through Weston and the N.I.C.E. and shows how the human race can destroy itself if we use science to replace nature.

Lewis implants these ideas into his third volume in the Space trilogy. Bentness is defined in *That Hideous Strength* with the

7. Schwartz, *Final Frontier*, 6.

8. Bolton, "Battling That Hideous Strength," 5.

9. Bolton, "Battling That Hideous Strength," 6.

10. Bolton, "Battling That Hideous Strength," 4.

11. Bolton, "Battling That Hideous Strength," 1–3.

increasing dependence and the abuse of scientific technology, "almost totally in the hands of those leading a vast global conspiracy to rob humans of their personhood."[12] Weston, Wither, and Alcasan become "un-manned" or robbed of what makes them uniquely human. Using technology to make humans the dominant race in our section of outer space, above all the other sentient beings throughout the planets around us, is a disruption of the natural Order of Being. Changing our own place in the Cosmic Hierarchy is wrong if we do not wait to be deified in God's own time.[13] Immortality is a reward for our obedience, and Lewis likens that reward to the consummation of obedience.[14] Humans are meant to be deified, and that potential is already inside us; if we succeed in our obedience, God will put us in our proper place as "pillars of God's temple."[15] Lewis also explains that there is no such thing as an "ordinary" person since humans already have the potential for deification.[16] God's intention is to perfect humans as long as we put ourselves entirely in God's will.[17]

Further, Lewis's human characters plan to usurp any and all other planets, using up all the resources available before moving on to a fresh planet. Weston's actions clearly reflect Western colonialism, especially when we hear Weston's plans for Malacandra. Monika B. Hilder rightly states, "As his name suggests, Weston represents the height of Western humanism, or rather its demise in the amoral 'new man,' the Nietzschean superman."[18] Weston's intent is to jump from planet to planet, exhausting resources in order to immortalize the human species. He goes as far as telling the Oyarsa of Malacandra that he would gladly colonize other planets at the expense of their alien inhabitants in order to immortalize

12. Downing, *Planets in Peril*, 145.

13. Mosley, *Being Deified*, 9.

14. Lewis, "The Weight of Glory," 2.

15. Lewis, "The Weight of Glory," 2–5.

16. Lewis, "The Weight of Glory," 9.

17. Lewis, *Mere Christianity*, 207.

18. Hilder, *Surprised by the Feminine*, 71.

the human race.[19] Weston has Ransom translate the following for the Oyarsa:

> I am prepared without flinching to plant the flag of man on the soil of Malacandra: to march on, step by step, superseding, where necessary, the lower forms of life that we find, claiming planet after planet, system after system, till our posterity—whatever strange form and yet unguessed mentality they have assumed—dwell in the universe wherever the universe is habitable.[20]

As the conversation between Weston, Ransom, and Oyarsa continues, Oyarsa reveals that what bent humans like Weston fear most is Death. He says, "It is the Bent One, the lord of your world, who wastes your lives and befouls them with flying from what you know will overtake you in the end. If you were subjects of Maleldil you would have peace."[21] The return to Maleldil is universal. Some may call it Death, but Maleldil's beings do not necessarily have to die in order to return to their Creator. Ransom, for example, returns to Perelandra where he will be healed of the wound in his foot from the Un-man and presumably live forever.[22] Merlin also returns to Maleldil after the descent of the gods, at which time his "final severance from the body [is] near."[23] The separation of Merlin's body and soul does not necessarily mean Death, but more likely a liberation of his soul. It makes no difference whether or not the human race hops from planet to planet because everything and everyone will return to Maleldil at some point. Fear of reuniting with Maleldil is simply ignorance; Maleldil is the Creator in Lewis's fiction, and fear of returning to Maleldil would be irrational. Weston's description of moving to new planets once the resources are exhausted lacks all moral concern for the beings of other planets. Lewis's message is that the human race puts itself above all other life forms and disregards each planet's eldila and

19. Lewis, *Out of the Silent Planet*, 136.
20. Lewis, *Out of the Silent Planet*, 136.
21. Lewis, *Perelandra*, 139.
22. Lewis, *That Hideous Strength*, 366.
23. Lewis, *That Hideous Strength*, 324.

Oyarses. This anthropocentric mindset disrupts the natural Cosmic Hierarchy throughout the planets that humans colonize, and Lewis presents this message by reminding humans of Christianity's natural place in space.

Alongside anthropocentrism is evolutionism, which Lewis includes in the N.I.C.E.'s crusade against mortality. Evolutionism is a philosophy that consists of all the theories of evolution as a whole, "projecting Darwinism into the metaphysical sphere."[24] The N.I.C.E.'s pseudo-scientists in the trilogy carry out multiple experiments such as the Head in order to find a way to immortalize the human race and improve evolution. Mark Studdock, sociologist and amateur writer for the N.I.C.E., originally helps this organization in their goals to obtain Bragdon Wood. He gradually realizes that he is part of a more sinister operation and eventually finds the area where animals are kept for vivisection and other experimentation.[25] Near the end of the text, scientist Filostrato is decapitated with his own device made for murdering other victims for the scientific use of their heads.[26] In response to these events and experiments, Downing states that Lewis "began the trilogy as a deliberate critique of what he called evolutionism . . . speculating that humankind may eventually evolve into its own species of divinity, jumping from planet to planet and star to star."[27] Michael Travers similarly explains that "it is the union of eugenics and technology that makes man's self-abolition possible, and the Third Reich represented that possibility all too obviously for Lewis in 1943."[28] It is quite possible that Lewis wrote THS with eugenics in mind, having read G. K. Chesterton's essay on eugenics in 1926.[29] Even later, in "Religion and Rocketry," Lewis wrote that humans destroy and dominate wherever and whenever we can.[30] He argues, "Man

24. Downing, *Planets in Peril*, 14.

25. Lewis, *That Hideous Strength*, 100.

26. Lewis, *That Hideous Strength*, 352.

27. Downing, *Planets in Peril*, 36.

28. Travers, "Free to Fall," 119.

29. Heck, "Uncommon Truth in Common Language," 391.

30. Lewis, "Religion and Rocketry," 4–5.

destroys or enslaves every species he can. Civilized man murders, enslaves, cheats, and corrupts savage man."[31] Arguably because of his personal religious and moral beliefs, Lewis's concern here passes directly into his science fiction work with Weston's plan to invade other planets for unlimited human resources. Downing also explains that Lewis was afraid evolution was catching on with the "popular imagination." Dominating others, becoming immortal, and putting humankind on the same level as God, are all warnings embodied in Weston and the Un-man.[32]

Devine, Wither, Straik, Fairy Hardcastle, and others from the N.I.C.E., create artificial means to keep humans alive by separating the mind from the living body. They trick scientists into replacing God with highly evolved versions of men by abusing eugenics and technology; the scientist Filostrato reanimates Alcasan's head, which is inhabited by a dark eldil. In the context of Lewis's time, the Ransom trilogy connects Weston's ideas of domination and the goals of the N.I.C.E. with Hitler's dream of the *Übermensch*. Filostrato tells Mark that he looks "forward to a world of perfect purity."[33] He continues to ask, "What are the things that most offend the dignity of man? Birth and breeding and death. How if we are about to discover that man can live without any of the three"?[34] His questions directly correlate to evolutionary concerns during WWII with the focus on purifying the human race. At this historical point in time, humans possess the technology to manipulate the way we evolve by weeding out the imperfections and reaching perfection over time. The N.I.C.E.'s reanimation of severed heads echoes some of the ideas and rumored medical experiments of the Nazis.[35] For example, Dr. Josef Mengele, famously dubbed the "Angel of Death," experimented on Holocaust prisoners and is known to have used Gypsy children as subjects for his experiments. He studied the children, both alive and deceased, preserved their

31. Lewis, "Religion and Rocketry," 4.

32. Downing, *Planets in Peril*, 36.

33. Lewis, *That Hideous Strength*, 171.

34. Lewis, *That Hideous Strength*, 171.

35. Downing, *Planets in Peril*, 54.

organs, and in some instances preserved their heads for further study.[36] While no information is given on whether Mengele experimented with reanimating any organs, Grace Ironwood's brief explanation of a failed German experiment in which someone tried to preserve a criminal's severed head may have been Lewis's reference to medical experiments similar to Mengele's.

Possessing and using this new technology in order to improve humanity's place in the Cosmic Hierarchy of Being can only result in the destruction of humanity itself. In *The Abolition of Man*, Lewis discusses how we can bring about our own extinction by artificially "improving" humans, which takes place in *That Hideous Strength*. He writes that the final evolution of humans destroys the race: "Man's final conquest has proved to be the abolition of man."[37] In other words, humans would no longer be humans after human nature (emotions, empathy, sympathy, freedom of choice) is lost in the evolutionary process. During the trial at Meldilorn, the Oyarsa in *OSP* makes clear to Weston that humans would no longer be humans if evolved.[38] In *THS*, Wither and the scientists go to great lengths to perfect the reanimation of Alcasan's head and introduce the Head as the first successful immortal being, not to mention the "new" image of God. Of course, it is only immortal because the Head is preserved by chemicals and tubes and inhabited by an evil eldil.[39] The scientists' success is an example of humanity bringing about its own demise. Alcasan (or more truly, his head) can no longer experience human emotions, free will, or have a meaningful relationship with other humans. Striving to be immortal through scientific means disrupts the natural Cosmic Hierarchy and negates humanity and all the experiences and emotions unique to humans.

One of Lewis's purposes in his trilogy was to warn against the misuse of science. Michael Travers examines Lewis's *Abolition of Man* and concludes that WWII forced the British people to think

36. Levine, "Nazi Medical Experimentation."
37. Lewis, *Abolition of Man*, 64.
38. Lewis, *Out of the Silent Planet*, 137.
39. Lewis, *That Hideous Strength*, 182.

about scientific morals, specifically of the Third Reich: "The early 1940s were also the war years when many Britons faced difficulties brought about by the war and were forced to consider the serious metaphysical and ethical questions raised by Nazi aggression."[40] Travers alludes to the scientific experiments carried out in concentration camps with the purpose of creating the *Übermensch*. During the early 1940s Lewis published *OSP* (1938), *The Problem of Pain* (1940), gave his *Mere Christianity* broadcasts (1941–1944, published in 1952), *The Screwtape Letters* (1942), *The Abolition of Man* (1943) . . . and *THS* in 1945, calling it a "tall story" about the "serious point" he made in *The Abolition of Man*.[41] Lewis's work over these years focuses primarily on scientific and religious morals and their effects on future generations. By using outer space to present scientific and religious morals, readers are given a chance to view our actions from a different perspective, which we will discuss further.

Abusing science can cause the downfall of humanity without the consent of future generations, which may not agree with the scientific progress made in the present day. If we develop "the power to make [our] descendants what [we please]," or a race that is truly a master human race, all the generations that come after are really submissive to it.[42] Lewis clarifies his meaning when he explains that "each new power won *by* man is a power over man as well. Each advance leaves him weaker as well as stronger."[43] As humans improve their sciences and technologies, they grow in knowledge; on the other hand, they also become more dependent upon those technologies, and there is the potential that scientific creations will become unmanageable. The N.I.C.E. creates a power they cannot control, and they begin to envy the Head's immortality.[44] Envying their creation only causes the scientists to become more preoccupied with trying to make immortality possible for

40. Travers, "Free to Fall," 108.
41. Travers, "Free to Fall," 108.
42. Lewis, *Abolition of Man*, 57.
43. Lewis, *Abolition of Man*, 58.
44. Lewis, *Abolition of Man*, 66.

more humans, despite the fact that they destroy humanity in the process and future generations might not agree with their decisions. Travers argues that the disconnect between generations is another disruption in the Chain of Being, or what Lewis calls the *Tao*:

> It limits the options of later generations by making choices for its own benefit, rather than passing on the heritage of traditional morality that so many generations of human beings have passed on to their children. The conditioners will not pass on what they received from the *Tao* as their ancestors did for them . . . Rather, the conditioners will pass on a new understanding of morality, and this is a redefinition of humanity—or, more properly, the abolition of humanity as we know it.[45]

If we look at the members of the N.I.C.E., we see people creating what they please without giving thought to how future generations may receive it. The N.I.C.E. uses the power of Creation in order to make humans as *they* please.[46] If not for Ransom and the descent of the gods preventing the N.I.C.E.'s success, perhaps humanity in *THS* would have been doomed.

Moreover, Western colonization in the trilogy develops with human characters' relationships with alien characters. Like Downing's *Planets in Peril*, Schwartz discusses the struggle for existence, Western imperialism, and colonization in the trilogy. Specifically, Schwartz points out the struggle that Weston and Devine have with foreign intelligent beings. The men assume that the hrossa, séroni, and pfifltriggi mean to harm them simply because they are "other," or different from humans. Historically speaking, Western colonization comes to mind with the domination of, in my own context, Native American land and the lack of understanding (or communication in general) between European and Native American people. Similarly, the colonization of natives in Australia, India, and other countries depicts the same lack of understanding, communication, and the assumption that different cultures were

45. Travers, "Free to Fall," 120.
46. Lewis, *Abolition of Man*, 59.

barbaric because they were different, resulting in hostility and bloodshed. Weston and Devine symbolize Western imperialism in their beliefs on colonization and racial superiority.[47] The scientists are convinced they are more intelligent and powerful than all the other hnau on Malacandra simply because they are men and everyone else is different from them. Projecting this behavior in space gives the reader a new perspective of colonization as it occurs on Earth.

In *Out of the Silent Planet*, Weston's abuse of Harry, the original intended human sacrifice to the séroni, is an example of the unequal relationship between humans. Harry is the young boy at the beginning of *OSP* whom Weston and Devine plan to give to the séroni. They choose Harry primarily because he is an "idiot boy" and "incapable of serving humanity and only too likely to propagate idiocy."[48] The scientists dominate Harry because they are intellectual, but the real inequality and disruption of the Cosmic Hierarchy stems from how they treat him. Naturally, each individual has a unique spot in the Chain of Being, but Weston and Devine use Harry for their own gain. Their intent connects them with the Nazi ideals and eugenics movement of the early twentieth century, just as Downing connects parts of Hitler's agenda in creating the master race with the N.I.C.E. Harry's mother, Weston, and Devine describe Harry as slow, simple-minded, and therefore much lower in the hierarchy than the two scientists.[49] Weston even goes as far as to say that Harry was only "a preparation," and not up to his standards of a human, unlike Ransom who is more competent.[50] Schwartz explains that "these issues [of human hierarchy] were increasingly acute in the early twentieth century, when projects for the 'transformation of humanity' turned from speculative fictions into real-life legislative agendas for the improvement of the species, and at their most extreme, into lethal crusades to secure

47. Schwartz, *Final Frontier*, 22.

48. Lewis, *Out of the Silent Planet*, 12, 21.

49. Lewis, *Out of the Silent Planet*, 14.

50. Lewis, *Out of the Silent Planet*, 21.

the future of the evolutionary process itself."[51] Here, Schwartz also echoes Lewis's views from *The Abolition of Man* as discussed above.

Furthermore, Schwartz explains some of the Nazi objectives to manipulate the process of human evolution to make a master race. Camps such as Auschwitz and Chelmno gassed or shot large groups of Jews at once to cleanse the German population. The relationship between humans and the rest of the Cosmic Hierarchy changed tremendously at this time, just as Lewis's fictional world would have if the N.I.C.E. succeeded with its experiments. Generally, if humans evolved so drastically that they brought about their own extinction, the rest of the Cosmic Hierarchy would be severely affected; there would no longer be a bridge between God and non-sentient beings. One of humanity's roles is to shepherd animals, and without humans to bridge the gap, there would be too great a divide between God and smaller creations. Downing's *Planets in Peril* also connects Weston's ideas on evolution with the Nazi mindset. Downing states that Lewis feared that the general public idealized the natural process of evolution and the multiple theories that make up evolutionism. Schwartz takes this idea and adds the anti-colonization aspect in which Ransom fights against Weston's attempts to leapfrog the human race from planet to planet in order to survive indefinitely. In short, the World Wars and the accompanying anthropocentrism resulted in the image of mankind as villains.

Finally, the N.I.C.E.'s experiments result in a replacement for God. After the Head is introduced and the pseudo-scientists call it God, we find that the true purpose of Belbury is to create a means of immortality. Avoiding death is the ultimate disruption of natural order and allows humans to place themselves on an equal pedestal with God. In *THS*, Straik explains, "The resurrection of Jesus in the Bible was a symbol: tonight you shall see what is symbolised . . . we are offering you the unspeakable glory of being present at the creation of God Almighty . . . you shall meet the first sketch of the real God. It is a man—or a being made by man—who will

51. Schwartz, *Final Frontier*, 6.

finally ascend the throne of the universe. And rule forever."[52] Straik even tells Mark that he will be present at the "creation of God Almighty" when he is about to meet the Head for the first time.[53] The Head is an omniscient creation made by man, which is meant to "ascend the throne of the universe" by being resurrected and living indefinitely. The Head is "the first of the New Men"[54] and "the beginning of Man Immortal and Man Ubiquitous . . . Man on the throne of the universe."[55] Lewis's characters create a replacement for God, rather than obeying God and waiting to be deified.

Lewis's humans would be as gods, and in so doing they disrupt the Cosmic Chain by creating a means for indefinite life. Humans, and any other race or species, are simply not meant to live forever unless God deifies them. If we think back to *OSP*, Augray tells Ransom that "a world is not made to last forever, much less a race; that is not Maleldil's way."[56] Augray shows us Lewis's stance on WWII scientific morals; his message is that no race is meant to be immortal unless God gives them immortality. It is futile for humans to seek an alternative route to immortalize their presence in the universe. Living, sentient creatures will return to God in the same way each of Lewis's fictional races will return to Maleldil. That reunion is unavoidable, and certainly not to be feared. His science fiction trilogy allows his readers to see the results of scientific interference with evolution from the outer space perspective, and brings his message back to Earth in *THS*.

52. Lewis, *That Hideous Strength*, 174–76.

53. Lewis, *That Hideous Strength*, 176.

54. Lewis, *That Hideous Strength*, 174.

55. Lewis, *That Hideous Strength*, 175.

56. Lewis, *Out of the Silent Planet*, 100.

SIN IN SPACE?

The Meaning of Free Will
and the Importance of Choice

In Lewis's outer space, bentness and sin are portrayed in the same way as on Earth, allowing them to be accessible ideas to readers. "Bent" is the word the Oyarses and hnau use to describe sin. "Evil" in this context is unlike both bentness and sin; evil is the absence of good and existence. In his "Introduction to Athanasius' On the Incarnation," Lewis defends the saint's conviction that Christianity is a belief system to which humanity must return, and it is Athanasius who states that "evil is non-being, the negation and antithesis of good."[1] We cannot necessarily equate bentness with evil since in Lewis's view, bentness is unbelief and action-based, whereas evil is "non-being." Lewis does, on the other hand, describe the Un-man as evil, but he uses "evil" as the antithesis of good.

Lewis's Bent One is the name for Earth's Oyarsa, and its bentness stems from its desire to rule Thulcandra separately from Maleldil. The bentness of disrupting the natural cosmic order and disobeying Maleldil is not the only example of bentness that Lewis gives. David Downing explains that in *A Preface to Paradise Lost*, Lewis argues that one of the origins of sin is breaking the order of that chain: "With God at the top of the great chain . . . everyone and everything had a natural station, ruling over those below,

1. Athanasius, *On the Incarnation*, 9.

obeying those above. A great many sins, according to this conception, derive from not recognizing one's station, and thus perverting the natural order."[2] This is an internal cause for sin, in which the person becomes restless in their place in the chain and wishes to move up the hierarchy. In this way, according to the Ransom trilogy, humans become "bent." Ransom learns and understands that bentness can come from within one's own person in the desire for something other than what God gives us. That desire stems from the need for control; Ransom realizes this while he tries to explain earthly evil to the Green Lady on Perelandra.[3] The Unman in chapter 9 of *Perelandra* tries to explain the difference between experiencing the pleasure of everything Maleldil gives them and seeking goods other than that which is given in order to make Ransom look like the one who must be "made older."[4] Ransom is finally able to make Tinidril understand that we are given "a way to walk out of *our* will."[5] In other words, "bentness" in Lewis's work means choosing our own will over the will of Maleldil; Maleldil gives the hnau a chance to freely choose obedience to his will, and that free choice is a source of joy for hnau.

Ransom is faced with the same realization when he fails to find the fruit he was looking for and when he swims against the waves rather than letting the waves take him on their own course. He is frustrated when he does not have control over his situation, but eventually learns that he must relinquish his own control in order to fully accept his place under Maleldil.[6] Humans long for godlike control so they can ensure their own happiness, pleasure, and safety, but vulnerability is a necessary part of life.[7] Even though Ransom submits himself to Maleldil's will, he still needs to overcome his own desire for control.[8] In the Ransom sec-

2. Downing, "Rehabilitating H.G. Wells," 25.
3. Downing, *Planets in Peril*, 89.
4. Lewis, *Perelandra*, 98.
5. Lewis, *Perelandra*, 102.
6. Lewis, *Perelandra*, 127.
7. Downing, *Planets in Peril*, 38.
8. Downing, *Planets in Peril*, 37.

ondary world, as in Lewis's understanding of the primary world, hnau have their own free will and must freely choose the correct paths. If they choose rightly and choose Maleldil's will, they will be rewarded. On Perelandra, the key to closeness with Maleldil is giving oneself entirely to Maleldil's will. We see Ransom struggling against the waves while trying to swim to Tinidril's island, and no matter how hard he tries, he ends up back on the island where he started, only for both islands to connect during the night after he gives up swimming against the current.[9] Ransom would have made his way to Tinidril whether he fought the waves or simply let the waves take him where they would. Conversely on Earth, sometimes good can come from asserting one's will. For example, we may tell a lie in order to protect someone else, and that lie would serve our need and the need of the other person. On Perelandra, on the other hand, it seems that in all cases, one must freely give up one's will in order to connect with and obey Maleldil and reach goodness or reward. We see multiple times throughout *Perelandra* (as well as some of Lewis's essays) that bentness is affected by one's ability to make independent choices.

Tinidril, for instance, is the unfallen Eve figure on Perelandra. She is pure and innocent, and is able to remain so throughout the text even though she learns about the outside worlds from Ransom and the Un-man. Tinidril is a blank slate when it comes to the choices she makes; she is freely able to make her own choices, whether they are aligned with Maleldil's will or go against it. In his book-length examination of Lewis's fiction, *Planet Narnia*, Michael Ward explains how and why the Un-man tempts Tinidril: "He keeps attempting to poison her imagination (the first step in undermining her will) by telling her tales of tragic heroines who had been 'oppressed by fathers, cast off by husbands, deserted by lovers,' female martyrs who, if men had had their way, would have been kept down 'to mere childbearing.'"[10] The Un-man tries to affect Tinidril by telling her stories that may influence her choices. The images of oppressed women could cause her to resent Tor or

9. Lewis, *Perelandra*, 50.

10. Ward, *Planet Narnia*, 170.

choose her own independence over her devotion to Maleldil. The stories about powerful women may change her idea of childbearing and mothering Perelandra as a planet, and she may begin to see her feminine role as weak. His strategy is "to awaken in her mind not vanity concerning her physical beauty, but egoism concerning her beautiful soul."[11] Similarly, David Leigh explains that Ransom's job is to help Tinidril resist the Un-man's idea that her disobedience will actually "make her more like God, independent, self-creating, and beyond good and evil."[12] As Travers states in his essay "Free to Fall: The Moral Ground of Events on Perelandra," she is "a creature 'innocent' of sin [with] a legitimate free choice to fall or not to fall."[13] Tinidril is free to make her own choices, and therefore free to choose wrongly.

Lewis further discusses the importance of choice and free will in *Mere Christianity*. In this text, which was originally contemporary to *Perelandra*, he explores how each person is gifted with their own independence and ability to choose freely to either submit to God's will or live separately. On free will, good, and evil, Lewis writes, "Free will, though it makes evil possible, is also the only thing that makes possible any love or goodness or joy worth having."[14] Although the ability to make one's own choices allows for making the wrong choice, it is necessary in order for humans to fully experience love. He continues to explain that if all humans were only able to make either all good choices or all evil ones, the world would not be worth God's creation.[15] Lewis continues to write that "the happiness which God designs for His higher creatures is the happiness of being freely, voluntarily united to Him and to each other in an ecstasy of love and delight compared with which the most rapturous love between a man and a woman on this earth is mere milk and water."[16] Essentially, it is a *choice* to

11. Ward, *Planet Narnia*, 170.
12. Travers, "Free to Fall," 257.
13. Travers, "Free to Fall," 145.
14. Lewis, *Mere Christianity*, 48.
15. Lewis, *Mere Christianity*, 48.
16. Lewis, *Mere Christianity*, 48.

sacrifice one's own independent will and submit to the will of God, because neither humans nor God would find joy if a choice was forced upon us.

God wants happiness for all his creations, but one pervading question is how God can allow evil to happen, or allow his creations to become bent. Answering one of Arthur Greeves's letters on September 12, 1933 regarding how God could understand human evil Lewis wrote, "Evil itself is simply a corruption of good. God not only understands but shares the desire for complete happiness. The difference is that we as human beings try to obtain that happiness in the wrong way. God knows the only way we can obtain it, and is merciless in trying to lead us to that good end in the right way."[17] Again, humans must have their own free will so they can choose to follow God. Voluntarily choosing God brings both humans and God ultimate happiness. But Lewis also discusses how humans may choose wrongly: "What Satan put into the heads of our ancestors was the idea that they could 'be like gods'—could set up on their own as if they had created themselves—be their own masters—invent some sort of happiness for themselves outside God, apart from God."[18] The Un-man tries to do exactly this to Tinidril; he tries to persuade her to become her own master and make her own happiness by fulfilling her own desires. But Tinidril chooses to act under Maleldil's will and avoids becoming bent, unlike the earthly Adam and Eve. Tinidril and Maleldil find mutual happiness because Tinidril freely and voluntarily submits to Maleldil's will. Ransom also finds that he is free to choose whether he returns back to Thulcandra or stays on Malacandra in *OSP*, and that he has the choice to follow Maleldil's wishes to leave the fixed island at night.

We must now consider how the Un-man is affected by free will. When Weston was still entirely alive and human, he chose not to accept the Christian God. As we already discussed, his intent to colonize and dominate are bent choices. But Weston is unmanned, and the Un-man's choices are truly bent. The dark spirit

17. Hooper, *War in Deep Heaven*, 121–26.
18. Lewis, *Mere Christianity*, 49.

that inhabits Weston's body is a fallen eldil—a higher being than humans in the hierarchy. Downing argues that "the Bent One (Lucifer) was granted one of the greatest of all goods—to be Maleldil's viceroy over a world. Yet he would accept no sovereign over him, considering equality with Maleldil as a thing to be grasped. And the temptation to which he fell becomes one he will tempt humans with, to become gods unto themselves."[19] Whether the Un-man is the Bent One or one of its inferiors is a minor detail; either way, the spirit was granted the privilege of taking care of one of Maleldil's worlds, but chose to take advantage of that powerful position.

Lewis further claims in *Mere Christianity* that the higher up in the hierarchy a being is, the stronger the effect of their choice. For example, Lewis asks why God would create a creature with the ability to choose wrongly, because in doing so God also creates bentness. His answer is that "the better stuff a creature is made of—the cleverer and stronger and freer it is—then the better it will be if it goes right, but also the worse it will be if it goes wrong . . . an ordinary man, still more so; a man of genius, still more so; a superhuman spirit best—or worst—of all."[20] Additionally, Lewis explains in *The Abolition of Man* that "it is the magician's bargain: give up our soul, get power in return. But once our souls, that is ourselves, have been given up, the power thus conferred will not belong to us. We shall in fact be the slaves and puppets of that to which we have given our souls."[21] Weston experiences this exactly—he gives up his self-will and becomes subject to the dark Force he calls into his body. Weston, if he had prevailed, could have done a great amount of good on Perelandra, according to Lewis's connection between power and choice. The Un-man, of course, is bent in the sense of being deprived of goodness; the spirit or eldil that becomes the Un-man has a greater impact with its choices than the human Weston could because it was originally higher in the Cosmic Hierarchy.

19. Downing, *Planets in Peril*, 39.
20. Lewis, *Mere Christianity*, 49.
21. Lewis, *Abolition of Man*, 72.

There must be some significance behind bent actions coming from a character who has been un-manned and separated from what makes him human. On one hand, Ransom's role is to protect Tinidril; he chooses to do everything he can to prevent the Un-man from succeeding (despite his self-doubt), and he reflects Christ as the savior of the planet.[22] Maleldil tests Ransom in his belief by giving him that task. Ransom feels like he cannot overtake the Un-man physically or emotionally, yet still tries to carry out Maleldil's wishes.[23] Ransom is endowed with the same free will of all sentient beings and chooses to continue fighting the Un-man. On Malacandra, Ransom's task is to "overcome his habitual fearfulness; his great task on [Perelandra is] to overcome his habitual willfulness, to acknowledge this pressure as a Presence and to submit to a will greater than his own."[24] Weston, on the other hand, voluntarily renounces his control over his own will, but invites the dark spirit into his body. Weston says, "I, Weston, am your God and your Devil. I call that Force into me completely."[25] The "Force" refers to the Force of the Devil, and Jared Lobdell reiterates that Weston "invites the force into him, and is unmanned. He becomes, in fact, the Un-Man—is taken over by a devil, perhaps the Devil."[26] If we think back to Weston's original intentions, he tries to control and secure the future of the human race. He is willing to move humans to different planets in order to prolong their time in the universe. Unlike Ransom, who relinquishes his control and, as Downing states, gains "complete self-surrender," Weston tries to gain control over the future of humanity, which is not meant to be controlled by any other being than Maleldil.[27] By bringing free will and the potential for humans to become bent into outer space, Lewis provides his readers with a reflection of our own free will

22. Downing, *Planets in Peril*, 52.

23. Schwartz, *Final Frontier*, 80.

24. Downing, *Into the Region of Awe*, 95.

25. Lewis, *Perelandra*, 82.

26. Lobdell, *The Scientifiction Novels*, 90.

27. Downing, *Into the Region of Awe*, 105.

and how the choices we make on Earth affect our relationship with God.

RECOVERING OUTER SPACE
AND CHRISTIANITY

Projecting humanity and recovering the Christian worldview in outer space allows Lewis to give his readers a new perspective of our own actions on Earth. He draws numerous connections to Christianity in his texts, and many of the images he includes in Malacandra and Perelandra are religious. Tinidril and Tor, for example, serve as images of Adam and Eve on Perelandra. Lewis's hierarchical Chain of Being is strikingly similar to the Christian hierarchy in which God is at the top and humans below. These connections are not simply allegorical; they have a specific purpose and present his readers with images of how humans must treat religion, or belief. If we connect his interplanetary novels with Tolkien's idea of Escape and Recovery, Lewis's audience is able to Recover the ideas of nature, outer space, and religion as it is meant to be on Earth.

Tolkien's essay "On Fairy-Stories" explains Escape as one of the three things fiction, more specifically fantasy and fairy-stories, provides for readers. He does not mean Escape in the "desertion" sense, running away in cowardice;[1] rather Tolkien describes Escape from things such as "hunger, thirst, poverty, pain, sorrow, injustice, death,"[2] which are elements humans can experience during war. Tolkien introduces the ultimate Escape as the Escape from

---

1. Tolkien, "On Fairy-Stories," 148.
2. Tolkien, "On Fairy-Stories," 151.

Death.[3] His fiction provides the Great Escape through elves and their immortality, whereas Lewis's N.I.C.E. tries to create human immortality through science. Escaping from Death is an idea pertinent to Lewis's time and the World Wars as demonstrated by the Third Reich and the *Übermensch*, and his N.I.C.E. separating the mind from the body to immortalize one's consciousness. By projecting his readers into space, Lewis provides Recovery of the normalcy preceding war through Escape.

Aside from the Escape from adversity and Death during war, Lewis also provides an Escape from human self-abolition through the trilogy as a whole. Looking back at WWII and Scientism as a cause of humanity's self-destruction, abusing science for our own gain will cause us to evolve to a point at which we lose the emotions, conscience, and relationships with others that make us human. Bruce L. Edwards examines this idea of Escape, stating the following:

> What we may call "hyperrealism," Lewis called "sci-entism" or identified as a breed of "naturalism," and is his target in *The Abolition of Man*, *That Hideous Strength*, and *Miracles*; all three of these works prophesy the de-mise of the Enlightenment and its subsequent dissolu-tion into various relativisms and constructionisms that cheat humanity out of its humanness—that is, the image of God.[4]

This warning is not limited to *THS* because *OSP* and *Pere-landra* both deal with humanity's place in the Cosmic Chain. Ransom changes his mindset from wondering which hnau race controls the others to proving that he, as a human, is still a hnau creature.[5] If humans sever their connection with other beings, hnau or otherwise, and only focus on their own self-preservation, they will end up sacrificing that which makes them human. In oth-er words, using technology and the sciences to artificially enhance the human race will cause humanity's destruction. Lewis warns

3. Tolkien, "On Fairy-Stories," 153.

4. Edwards, "An Examined Life," 12.

5. Lewis, *Out of the Silent Planet*, 82.

his audience against dependence on eugenics and the technology mentioned above, and creating any scientific advance we cannot control. He uses space as an Escape from war-related hardships, but also uses it to allow his readers to reflect on how humanity ought to function.

Recovery is the second theme that Lewis describes in his Ransom trilogy after providing an Escape route from war for his readers. Tolkien explains that "Recovery . . . is a renewed vision of things that are familiar, a re-gaining of a clear view."[6] Fiction and fantasy literature allow readers to renew their vision of the mundane in order to regain their appreciation or awe of their own daily lives. Yes, Lewis and Tolkien write about talking animals, mythical creatures such as dwarves and elves, and rings and swords with special powers. But more importantly, these elements allow readers to experience the mundane from a new perspective. Recovering Christianity reminds us of the natural roles each being has in the universe, whether it be human, animal, or vegetable, and that every action affects the chain's relationship with God.

Nature, for instance, is part of that which is Recovered along with religion. Nature and its non-sentient creatures are indeed part of the Cosmic Hierarchy of Beings and part of the cosmic connection between God and all other creations. Lewis ends *THS* with the banquet at Belbury, where all the animals the scientists used for experiments escape and help destroy the N.I.C.E. "The banquet battle at Belbury Institute dramatizes resistance by the cosmic forces led by the ghost of Merlin and the captive animals who are rescued from vivisection," which proves that even nature must be left alone when it comes to its place in the Cosmic Chain in Lewis's fiction.[7] Nature retakes its position in the chain as the animals butcher the banquet guests.[8] Although non-sentient creatures are lower than humans on that chain, God does not mean for us to use them for our own selfish gain.[9]

6. Tolkien, "On Fairy-Stories," 146.

7. Travers, "Free to Fall," 261.

8. Lobdell, *The Scientifiction Novels*, 11.

9. Bolton, "Battling That Hideous Strength," 3.

Ransom experiences a Recovered image of space; Lewis gives new life to readers' idea of the dark, empty outer space and replaces it with an image of life and fullness. Ransom describes space as the heavens, neither dead space nor dark. He experiences space as directly connected with Christianity with added beauty and awe. When Ransom wakes up in his spaceship prison, he is amazed by what he sees out the window. He describes it as full of light.[10] It is not dark and empty, but filled with "planets of unbelievable majesty, and constellations undreamed of," which look like "celestial sapphires, rubies, emeralds and pin-pricks of burning gold" sparkling upon the fabric of "undimensioned, enigmatic blackness."[11] The stars are not simply "huge balls of flaming gas,"[12] but beautiful and colorful gems. Downing states: "It is an Edenic world of golden seas and lush tropical islands that float upon the waves . . . For Ransom this yearning, with both its pain and pleasure, seems 'sharp, sweet, wild, and holy, all in one.'"[13] Ransom is experiencing space as no one else knows it. Of course, at this point in *OSP* Ransom does not know that he is also in the presence of the eldila, but we learn that they are ever-present anyway. Space thrives with life in this way, contrary to the daily interpretation of it as barren. His vision of outer space as the place of Maleldil, or the heavens, shows us that outer space is directly connected to God and visually shows us what space truly is.

As for the Recovery of religion, Lewis accomplishes the renewal of Christianity by linking Maleldil with the Christian God. Simonson and Gilete, in their essay studying *The Chronicles of Narnia* and *The Lord of the Rings*, discuss Lewis's fantasy work as providing religious renewal for his readers. Lewis Recovers Christianity with "a fresh vision [that] leads not only to a new appreciation for the simple objects of the natural world, but also to the possibility of a new contact and relationship with the old,

---

10. Lewis, *Out of the Silent Planet*, 65.

11. Lewis, *Out of the Silent Planet*, 86.

12. Lewis, *Dawn Treader*, 522.

13. Lewis, *Out of the Silent Planet*, 91.

Christian message."[14] He shows us that Christianity is actually part of something larger spread across our planetary system. Maleldil and the Oyarses present readers with the possibility that we are a meaningful part of a larger whole rather than the only sentient beings in the universe. Lewis depicts Maleldil as validation for the Christian God, making God real and present for the reader. As Ransom experiences the epiphany that Maleldil and the Christian God are the same, we as readers are offered that same validation. According to Downing, "On Malacandra, Ransom gradually comes to realize that Maleldil was the same person as the God he already believed in."[15] In other words, Christianity is actually some readers' interpretation of the Creator and guardians in the greater cosmos as connected in the chart given in "Defining the Cosmic Hierarchy of Being and the Great Dance." Lewis subtly reminds us of our dormant religion by presenting Tor and Tinidril in human form. Since Maleldil took human form in Christ, that form is that which Maleldil, or "Reason," would take in any other world going forward.[16] Many readers may need reminding that humanity shares this physical connection with God. Our earthly beliefs only scratch the surface of something greater that extends out beyond our world.

The trilogy also allows readers to Recover their relationship with God. Tor and Tinidril are directly connected with Maleldil and even though they are Perelandra's equivalent of Adam and Eve, they are still (the Perelandrian equivalent of) humans who are faced with temptations. Downing writes that Tor and Tinidril's "unfallen state as creatures who have direct communication with their Creator and who enjoy a perfect union of their wills with his"[17] exemplifies humans in their unfallen state. As they become King and Queen of Perelandra, they are essentially given their own new level in Lewis's Cosmic Chain. They have obeyed Maleldil and as a result, Maleldil deifies them. Though they are hnau, they are

---

14. Simonson and Gilete, "*Chronicles of Narnia,*" 6.

15. Downing, *Planets in Peril*, 58.

16. Lewis, *That Hideous Strength*, 54.

17. Downing, *Into the Region of Awe*, 81.

given dominion over the planet and become the new Oyarses, as Perelandra was the planet's "foster mother."[18] Tor and Tinidril are charged with naming and shepherding all the beings and cultivating nature.[19] They have successfully left their roles as hnau and moved up the Cosmic Chain, but their new roles are given to them by Maleldil rather than taken for personal gain.

Lewis's outer space is the place of Maleldil, but Maleldil is not confined to outer space. Maleldil oversees everything in space by delegating the Oyarses to their planets, thus controlling each world through its Oyarsa. Further, Maleldil "remade the worlds before any world was made."[20] It is as if Maleldil went through a series of steps in the Great Dance before those worlds were ready to give to each Oyarsa. There can be no missteps, so any unexpected events such as the Bent One's disobedience must be folded in as part of the "Dance." Maleldil choreographs the Oyarses' steps so that they might counteract the Bent One's misstep. Maleldil acts through the Oyarses and Ransom to prevent the downfall of Perelandra. As Ransom begins to understand his role as "miracle" on Perelandra, Lewis writes, "One of the purposes for which He had done all this was to save Perelandra not through Himself but through Himself in Ransom. If Ransom refused, the plan, so far, miscarried."[21] Maleldil sets in motion a chain of actions that lead up to Ransom coming to Perelandra. As the creator and overseer, Maleldil is also the root of religion. Everything in the universe begins with Maleldil and ultimately returns to Maleldil upon death, since nothing that is created is meant to live forever.[22]

Outer space is the go-between of the planets for Maleldil, Oyarses, and eldila;[23] they live in the heavens whereas humans live on Earth. Space is not a sea of empty darkness with a few stars and planets here and there, or just the thriving vastness of "celestial

18. Lewis, *Perelandra*, 177.
19. Lewis, *Perelandra*, 177.
20. Lewis, *Perelandra*, 189.
21. Lewis, *Perelandra*, 123.
22. Lewis, *Out of the Silent Planet*, 100.
23. Downing, *Into the Region of Awe*, 86.

sapphires" that Ransom sees, but also Maleldil's place of existence. Maleldil is Lewis's portrait of the Christian God, the creator of the universe. Maleldil does not actually *live*, per se, in space, but simply exists there, making outer space the exact opposite of barren and empty.[24] Hnohra explains, "He is not that sort . . . that has to live anywhere."[25] Maleldil is in all things. The Oyarses and eldila are constantly present in the vast expanse between the stars and planets. Though humans may not always see these extraterrestrial beings, they are present nonetheless. The Oyarsa of Malacandra explains that he is not "here" in the same way that Ransom is "here" on that planet. The planets are just places in the heavens and Ransom cannot comprehend the rest.[26] The fictional Lewis, or the narrator named Lewis in the text, is also taught that Oyarses are not the sort to wait because they cannot have that type of experience. Ransom does not try to explain the details further and the fictional Lewis leaves the explanation there.[27] The eldila, or equivalent of the Christian angels, are also ever-present in space. Before Ransom departs from Malacandra, the Oyarsa in *OSP* confides in Ransom that "the eldila of deep heaven will be about [his] ship till it reaches the air of Thulcandra, and often in it" and will prevent Weston and Devine from killing him.[28] He also hears their subtle sounds and vibrations during his journey home.[29] Christianity as well as outer space is given new life in the Ransom trilogy; humans can experience life and the Christian worldview as it should be on Earth.

24. Lewis, *Out of the Silent Planet*, 69.

25. Lewis, *Out of the Silent Planet*, 69.

26. Lewis, *Out of the Silent Planet*, 119.

27. Lewis, *Perelandra*, 26.

28. Lewis, *Out of the Silent Planet*, 141.

29. Lewis, *Out of the Silent Planet*, 145.

WHAT DOES "RECOVERY" MEAN
FOR MODERN HUMANS?

There is plenty of evidence that Lewis was concerned about the future of the human race based on his recorded opinions of Hitler, the Third Reich, and the abuse of science and technology. He was concerned about the replacement of God. Lewis provides Escape from these things by bringing his readers out into space and allowing us to look at our world from the outside. According to Michael Ward, Lewis felt that any developments made in space exploration would end poorly based on historical events. Lewis observed that each time humans conquered a new land, it resulted in suffering and pain for the natives of that land.[1] Ward's footnote in this section also indicates that Neil Armstrong landed on the moon after Lewis died, leaving Lewis's reaction to the moon-landing a mystery.[2] Given his personal opinions regarding space travel and exploration, we can assume Lewis would have looked at humans' arrival on the Moon in the same way. Indeed, in "Religion and Rocketry" Lewis explains, "Against [alien life] we shall, if we can, commit all the crimes we have already committed against creatures certainly human but differing from us in features and pigmentation; and the starry heavens will become an object to which good men can look up only with feelings of intolerable guilt, agonized pity, and burning shame."[3] In his opinion, humans

1. Ward, *Planet Narnia*, 124.
2. Ward, *Planet Narnia*, 124.
3. Lewis, "Religion and Rocketry," 5.

would continue to pillage and ruin the lands of whatever planets they landed on if space travel became a success. Even still, one of Lewis's purposes in writing the Space trilogy may have been to explore and experiment with his reader's perspective of current events. By projecting us into space, Lewis introduces us to an alien perspective of humanity, and thus a Christian perspective on what it means to be human.

The creatures, sentient and non-sentient, that Ransom, Weston, and Devine meet while in space are aliens in that they are not of our own planet. They are what Alfred Kracher dubs "Meta-humans," or beings that allow us to look at ourselves from the outside.[4] His term is similar to "metacognition," or thinking about thinking; in Lewis's texts, humanlike beings observe humanity. Kracher claims that "the godlike [aliens] can sometimes tell us what to do or at least instruct us how to become better. The humanlike [aliens] teach us something about ourselves, too, but not by instruction; they teach by example—sometimes a bad example that we ought *not* to follow."[5] The Oyarses and eldila are the godlike aliens who teach humans through their own example and belief. The séroni teach Ransom (and through him, Lewis's readers) that there must be some sort of governing hierarchy between beings, and the reason why Earth is in its fallen state is because we have a bent Oyarsa. An old sorn explains, "There must be rule, yet how can creatures rule themselves? Beasts must be ruled by hnau and hnau by eldila and eldila by Maleldil. These creatures have no eldila. They are like one trying to lift himself by his own hair—or one trying to see over a whole country when he is on a level with it."[6] Conversely, the Un-man is the example humans are meant not to follow as he needlessly tortures and kills the frog-like creatures on Perelandra.[7] This is part of the answer to why Lewis reminds us of religion's natural place in space; readers are able to observe themselves through a new perspective, looking from the outside

4. Kracher, "Meta-Humans and Metanoia," 331.

5. Kracher, "Meta-Humans and Metanoia," 335.

6. Lewis, *Out of the Silent Planet*, 102.

7. Lewis, *Perelandra*, 93–95.

in, and are given examples of the right and wrong ways of living. Lewis's meta-human characters and their own beliefs in Maleldil teach us that a transition must be made from religious acts such as going to church and prayer to unwavering selfless belief.

Lewis was also concerned that the general moral code or the right way of living would be overrun by Scientism and technological advances. Perry C. Bramlett claims that Lewis saw religion as more of a way of life, a worldview, not bound to rituals such as going to church or praying before bedtime.[8] At the time, improving human life with technology brought about by WWII warfare was a popular mindset, rather than religious morals or the church. Perhaps people at the time even questioned religion because of the war, which may have fueled Lewis's BBC broadcasts that eventually became *Mere Christianity*.[9] The radio broadcasts were one way in which he could share his Christian morals with the people, but his fiction was another way—the same ideas he spoke about in his *Mere Christianity* broadcasts are presented again in his Ransom stories. In any case, Lewis believed that space exploration and the sciences and technology that accompany it could pose a threat to religion, as demonstrated in "Religion and Rocketry." The online journal *The Space Review* restates his views that he was "opposed to space exploration. He saw it as a substitute for religion and, for some people today, it is."[10] Since humans first landed on the Moon, scientists explore further and further away from Earth. Dinerman continues to explain:

> Today building a "spacefaring civilization" is closer than ever. In March 2006 George W. Bush's science advisor, John Marburger, spoke of bringing the solar system into 'humanity's economic sphere of influence.' There is every reason to believe that by the end of the twenty-first century a number of industries, from tourism to mining,

8. Bramlett, "Reluctant Convert," 105.

9. Heck, "Uncommon Truth in Common Language," 54.

10. Dinerman, "Then and Now," 2.

energy, and specialized manufacturing, will thrive outside the Earth's atmosphere.[11]

Lewis was at least correct that space exploration would become another historical example of humanity conquering foreign
lands, if we do indeed reach the point at which human industries
move outside our home planet.

With all this information in mind, let us now turn back to
the main question: why else does Lewis remind us of Christianity's place in outer space? Tolkien's Recovery aspect still holds true:
Lewis allows his readers to Recover outer space so we may then
Recover Christianity as it should be on Earth, but what should
Christianity mean to his readers? The application of Tolkien's "On
Fairy-Stories" should not stop at Escape and Recovery if we are
to answer these questions. Lewis gives his readers Christianity in
outer space as a means of providing Escape during WWII, thus
refocusing their concerns onto belief rather than religion. He
presents us with a new perspective to self-reflect and consider
ourselves from an outsider's point of view. His "meta-humans" re-
veal that it is not enough to carry out religious motions like prayer
and churchgoing. As far as we know, the hrossa, séroni, pfifltriggi,
and higher beings such as the eldila do not share similar religious
actions, rituals, or methods with us. Though the hnau have cer-
emonies such as the procession at Meldilorn on Malacandra and
the hunting of the hnakra on Perelandra, we do not experience
many more of their religious rituals, if there are any. Practicing a
religion means duty and obligation, and these things pervade one's
lifestyle. Ransom learns that one must wholeheartedly believe in
God and that belief pervades into the person's outlook on life and
way of living. Tolkien states, "Few lessons are taught more clearly
in [fairy-stories] than the burden of that kind of immortality, or
rather endless serial living, to which the 'fugitive' would fly."[12]

At the time of its publication, *OSP* was the first step in Lewis's
attempt at refocusing his readers from WWII to Christianity, in

11. Dinerman, "Then and Now," 3.
12. Tolkien, "On Fairy-Stories," 153.

which they could find relief for all of war's hardships. Lewis provided his readers with a Recovery of Christian faith in the face of tragedy that humanity created for itself. Woody Wendling expresses that Lewis's role as author of the trilogy allowed him to deliver a "change of consciousness" to readers.[13] His concern for the sciences replacing religion are voiced in Downing's essay "Rehabilitating H.G. Wells": "The realisation that thousands of people in one form or another depend on some hope of perpetuating and improving the human species for the whole meaning of the universe—that a 'scientific' hope of defeating death is a real rival to Christianity."[14] Similarly, Charles Moorman states that Lewis wrote *OSP* and introduced the idea of Earth as a Silent Planet to "create and maintain a metaphor that will serve to carry in fictional form the basic tenets of Christianity and present them from a non-Christian point of view, but without reference to normal Christian symbols."[15] Though the emphasis here is on religion, Lewis's trilogy places more emphasis on belief instead, bringing religion to a higher level.

In writing his Space trilogy, Lewis provides the Recovery of Christianity for his readers through Escape into outer space and adjusts his readers' focus from religion to belief and the right way of living. The hnau's unwavering faith and belief in Maleldil causes their religious actions to be bound with their lifestyle and worldview. Ransom's conversation with Hyoi in chapter 12 of *OSP*, for example, depicts the hrossa appreciating life and living in the moment rather than in their memories or desires. Hyoi explains that "every day in a life fills the whole life with expectation and memory and . . . these are that day,"[16] meaning that they take each experience as a unique event to be cherished, not repeated. It is similar to the idea that one must be pleased with what is given rather than go looking for what one desires; every experience is given by Maleldil, and honoring those experiences is the right way

13. Wendling and Wendling, "Angelic Hierarchy," 7.

14. Downing, "Rehabilitating H.G. Wells," 15.

15. Downing, "Rehabilitating H.G. Wells," 16–17.

16. Lewis, *Out of the Silent Planet*, 75–76.

of living. Likewise, everything Tinidril does is with Maleldil in mind. She says that she always walks with him, and that "to walk out of His will is to walk into nowhere."[17] To Lewis's hnau, Maleldil is a constant presence in their lives and they are directly connected to their Creator. Maleldil defines their way of living. As "meta-humans," Lewis's creatures, hnau and otherwise, reflect humans and our interrelationships with other earthly beings. In order to preserve our own race, humans must follow the Cosmic Chain of Being because it is our direct connection with God.

17. Lewis, *Perelandra*, 100.

BIBLIOGRAPHY

Athanasius. *On the Incarnation.* Coptic Orthodox Church Network, 1999. http://copticchurch.net//topics/theology/incarnation_st_athanasius.pdf.

Bolton, Cherish Asha. "Battling That Hideous Strength: C.S. Lewis on Morality, State, and Civil Society in Britain During the Second World War." Academia.edu, 2011. http://www.academia.edu/1211155/Battling_That_Hideous_Strength_C.S._Lewis_on_Morality_State_and_Civil_Society_in_Britain_During_the_Second_World_War.

Bramlett, Perry C. "Lewis the Reluctant Convert: Surprised by Faith." In *C.S. Lewis: Life, Works, and Legacy,* edited by Bruce L. Edwards, vol. 1. Westport, CT: Praeger, 2007.

Dinerman, Taylor. "C.S. Lewis and His Space Trilogy, Then and Now." *The Space Review,* Jan 10, 2011.

Downing, David C. *Into the Region of Awe: Mysticism in C.S. Lewis.* Downers Grove: InterVarsity, 2005.

———."Perelandra: A Tale of Paradise Retained." In *C.S. Lewis: Life, Works, and Legacy,* edited by Bruce L. Edwards, 2:35–51. Westport, CT: Praeger, 2007.

———. *Planets in Peril: A Critical Study of C.S. Lewis's Ransom Trilogy.* Amherst, MA: University of Massachusetts Press, 1992.

———. "Rehabilitating H.G. Wells: C.S. Lewis's Out of the Silent Planet." In *C.S. Lewis: Life, Works, and Legacy,* edited by Bruce L. Edwards, 2:13–34. Westport, CT: Praeger, 2007.

———. "That Hideous Strength: Spiritual Wickedness in High Places." In *C.S. Lewis: Life, Works, and Legacy,* edited by Bruce L. Edwards, 2:53–70. Westport, CT: Praeger, 2007.

Edwards, Bruce L. "An Examined Life." In *C.S. Lewis: Life, Works, and Legacy,* edited by Bruce L. Edwards, 1:1–15. Westport, CT: Praeger, 2007.

Heck, Joel D. "Mere Christianity: Uncommon Truth in Common Language." In *C.S. Lewis: Life, Works, and Legacy,* edited by Bruce L. Edwards, vol. 3. Westport, CT: Praeger, 2007.

Bibliography

Higgins, Sørina. "The Mythology of the Space Trilogy." *Islands of Joy* (blog), Oct 9, 2007. http://islandsofjoy.blogspot.com/2007/10/mythology-of-space-trilogy.html.

Hilder, Monika B. "Surprised by the Feminine: A Re-reading of Gender Discourse in C.S. Lewis's Perelandra." In *C. S. Lewis's Perelandra: Reshaping the Image of the Cosmos*, edited by Judith Wolfe and Brendan Wolfe, 69–82. Ohio: Kent State University Press, 2013.

Hooper, Walter. *War in Deep Heaven: The Space Trilogy of C. S. Lewis.* New York: Simon & Schuster, 1987.

Kracher, Alfred. "Meta-Humans and Metanoia: The Moral Dimension of Extraterrestrials." Academia.edu, 2006. https://www.academia.edu/2123922/Meta-humans_and_Metanoia_the_Moral_Dimension_of_Extraterrestrials.

Levine, Jason. "Auschwitz-Birkenau: Nazi Medical Experimentation." https://www.jewishvirtuallibrary.org/nazi-medical-experimentation-at-auschwitz-birkenau.

Lewis, C. S. *The Abolition of Man, or, Reflections on Education with Special Reference to the Teaching of English in the Upper Forms of Schools.* San Francisco: HarperSanFrancisco, 2001.

———. *The Discarded Image: An Introduction to Medieval and Renaissance Literature.* Cambridge: Cambridge University Press, 1964.

———. *God in the Dock: Essays on Theology.* Edited by Walter Hooper. London: Fount, 1979.

———. *Letters of C.S. Lewis.* Edited by Walter Hooper and W. H. Lewis. Orlando: Harcourt, 1993.

———. *Mere Christianity.* London: Bles, 1952.

———. *Out of the Silent Planet.* New York: Scribner, 2003.

———. *Perelandra.* New York: Scribner, 2003.

———. *A Preface to Paradise Lost.* Kolkata: Booksway, 2010.

———. *The Problem of Pain.* London: Centenary, 1940.

———. "Religion and Rocketry." *Scientific Integrity*, Apr 22, 2010.

———. *That Hideous Strength.* New York: Scribner, 2003.

———. *The Voyage of the Dawn Treader.* In The Chronicles of Narnia, edited by Pauline Baynes. New York: Harper Collins, 2001.

———. "The Weight of Glory." Sermon, Church of St. Mary the Virgin, Oxford, Jun 8, 1941.

Lobdell, Jared. *The Scientifiction Novels of C.S. Lewis: Space and Time in the Ransom Stories.* London: McFarland, 2004.

Mosley, David Russell. *Being Deified: Poetry and Fantasy on the Path to God.* Minneapolis: Fortress, 2016.

Pseudo-Dionysius. *The Celestial and Ecclesiastical Hierarchy of Dionysius the Areopagite.* London: Skeffington, 1894.

Schwartz, Sanford. *C.S. Lewis on the Final Frontier: Science and the Supernatural in the Space Trilogy.* Oxford: Oxford University Press, 2009.

Bibliography

Simonson, Martin, and Raúl Montero Gilete. "*The Chronicles of Narnia* and *The Lord of the Rings*: Similarities and Differences Between Two Children of the Great War." Vitória, Spain: Universidad del País Vasco, 2008. ler.letras. up.pt/uploads/ficheiros/4669.pdf.

Tolkien, J. R. R. "On Fairy-Stories." In *The Monsters and the Critics and Other Essays*, 109–61. Boston: Houghton Mifflin, 1984.

Travers, Michael. "Free to Fall: The Moral Ground of Events on Perelandra." In *C. S. Lewis's Perelandra: Reshaping the Image of the Cosmos*, edited by Judith Wolfe and Brendan Wolfe, 144–55. Ohio: Kent State University Press, 2013.

Tyson, Paul. "The Christian Platonism of Lewis and Tolkien." In *Returning to Reality: Christian Platonism for Our Times*, 21. Eugene, OR: Cascade, 2014.

Ward, Michael. *Planet Narnia: The Seven Heavens in the Imagination of C.S. Lewis*. Oxford: Oxford University Press, 2008.

Wendling, Susan, and Woody Wendling. "C.S. Lewis and the Angelic Hierarchy." *Inklings Forever* 8 (2012) 2–7. pillars.taylor.edu/inklings_ forever/vol8/iss1/27.

www.ingramcontent.com/pod-product-compliance
Lightning Source LLC
LaVergne TN
LVHW051712080426
835511LV00017B/2869